Raven Braids the Wind

Haiku: A Life in Syllables

Linda Toren

haiku o tsukuru hito
("a person who writes haiku")

Manzanita Writers Press

Raven Braids the Wind

Manzanita Writer's Press
San Andreas, CA
manzapress.com

ISBN: 978-0-9968858-6-7
Library of Congress: 2021925231

Author Photo: Jacob Toren
Cover art: *Windswept* by Wendy Rogers
(reproduced by permission of the artist)
Title page: *Raven* by Lian-Chai Toren
Text drawings: Theo Toren

Introduction

The first haiku I wrote was for an English assignment in sixth grade:

Lonely people live
within themselves like dusty
books upon a shelf.

That poem began my lifelong passion with poetry in general and haiku in particular. Until recently, I have faithfully followed the 5-7-5 format and written thousands of haiku. While teaching, I often wrote a haiku each day for my students. With fellow poet, Gary Thomas, we began a conversation in haiku which resulted in several self-published collections and inclusion in *Teaching With Fire (Poetry That Sustains the Courage to Teach)* by Sam M. Intrator & Megan Scribner, editors (2003).

In finding, reviewing and assembling the bibliography from my library, I realized I have haiku books dating back to 1958, many of them well-worn with yellowed pages. If ever there was a touchstone for me in poetry, it would be haiku.

I began writing a haiku-a-day in 2017. It has evolved into a diary of days. Rather than present it as a diary, I have captured poems from each month and present them here, embraced by the seasons.

Haiku is traditionally 5-7-5. For example, the word "haiku" itself counts as two syllables in English (hi-ku), but three sounds in Japanese (ha-i-ku). This isn't how "haiku" is said in Japanese, but it is how the syllables are counted.

Haiku Form

Most haiku use the formula of 5-7-5. The first and third lines each contain five syllables and the middle line contains seven. Some modern haiku use variations on this formula. Though compact in size, a haiku delivers a message. Some are humorous, while others make an observation or connect two opposing images.

After decades of writing haiku, I find I breathe the seventeen syllables—they inhabit my thoughts and other people's speech. I have begun "relaxing" the syllable count in service of flow and meaning.

The master of haiku is considered to be Matsuo Basho (1644-1694). He wrote about 1000 haiku poems through his lifetime, traveling around Japan. His chronicle *The Narrow Road to the Deep North* is the most famous haiku collection in Japan. His chronicle is actually a haibun—a combination of two poems: a prose poem or narrative and haiku. Following is his most cited verse.

Furuike ya
Kawazu tobikomo
Mizu no oto

Note the translation (Nobuyuki Yuasa):

Breaking the silence
Of an ancient pond,
A frog jumped into water—
A deep resonance.

The syllabic count does not work between languages. Thus, we can follow the count of 5-7-5 but as Yuasa commented "translation is a fearsome and humbling task."

The two books most influential to my understanding of haiku are *The Narrow Road to the Deep North and Other Travel Sketches* by Basho and *The Year of My Life* by Issa, both translated by Nobuyuki Yuasa.

This collection is based on daily haiku starting in 2019 and closing in 2020, the pandemic and political calamities constant markers in my thinking. There are two sections: haiku, focused on nature, and senryu, focused on human nature and internal thoughts. Note: Senryu may have seventeen syllables or fewer. An afterword shares haiku questions written in one day. The bibliography represents my personal collection of haiku books that have supported my understanding and work with haiku over many years.

Linda Toren
West Point, CA
Winter 2022

Acknowledgements

Thank you to my husband, Theo. His drawings punctuate the collection. His strong attunement to nature is a wonderful compliment to haiku.

True friends—Gary Thomas and Jim Jacobs lent their eagle eyes and fine poetic sense as readers of the first draft. Their feedback gave me the confidence to continue. Hope Satow assisted in the early stages of proofing.

One must belong to a community of writers, and I have been fortunate to be a part of "the licensed fools" for twenty-five years. You inspire me always.

Great thanks to Monika Rose—excellent editor and friend. Her advice and support made this publication possible.

Dedication

For my mother Laura Roslyn (1926-2017) & her father, my grandfather, En You Kau (1892-1970)

Pencil drawing by En You Kau

Contents

Spring

March

My orchid blooms
against a backdrop of
winter rainstorms.

Steady rain surges
sifts through cedars
thus purified.

Rushing water, an
effort to defy gravity—
I can dream-fly.

Deer munch the newly
hatched leaves of soap plants—
too green to resist.

Ravens wheel on cold
winds while a pileated
woodpecker tap, taps.

We saw the shadow
tree and made magic of it
because we noticed.

Daffodils nod their
heads in the greening breeze—
today is the day.

Spring. Tom turkeys talk,
fan their tails, walk in circles
while hens look for seeds.

Juncos play tag in
the golden bamboo as
towhees toss leaves.

The earth is spongy
with rain—creeks and rivulets
run past daffodils.

April

Rain measured in
inches then feet as rivers
cascade full of spring.

Trees whisper among
themselves—root to root—
about spring greens.

A red-tail hovers
then drops, tail feathers fanned,
straight to the ground.

The empty pasture
where you stood in the morning sun
is full of shadows.

Wild violas pinch
their purple-yellow faces
at the end of day.

Stellar's jays scream like
red-tail hawks, but I can tell
the difference.

To understand true
red, one need only look
at my tulips.

Hens chuck and squawk
about who is first on the nest—
so many eggs.

The earth, the earth, the
entire innocence of
the world.

Little mole lies on
the garden path while the cat
hides in the bamboo.

Weather turns
and still wisteria
cascade lavender.

May

Hairy woodpecker
taps, searches then drums a fine
rhythm—just to say.

Dogwood blossoms
open their palm petals
as if to pray.

I wish to be a
beetle deep in the yellow
glory of dandelions.

I saw the white
squirrel and assign it some
magical powers.

A raven calls—
cranky about blackbirds
on its tail.

Peony blossoms—
simple dark pink with golden
anthers—accept light.

Two hares—male and female
box like kangaroos.
She's not interested.

Each plant stretches its
roots, wakes from winter, hungry
for longer sunlight.

Red-tail turns, wheels on
the wind, snatches a blackbird
from thin air.

Petunias accept
snow—this cold touch of winter
so late in spring.

After rain smells like
the soul of the earth smiling
to itself.

Dry leaves speak a
private vocabulary
with shifting winds.

Our old goat stands on
a broken stump, surveying
how morning unfolds.

By nightfall bumble
bees love to sleep in lemon
blossoms.

Toad sits in the sun
outside a new-found home
it shares with lizard.

Raven returns,
chicken eggs and robbery.
Full of intention.

Summer

June

This is a good day
to count clouds, their cumulus
gray-white beauty.

Crickets count
moments of evening—
summer begins.

Molokai

A gecko calls once,
twice—tests the taste of
dark loneliness.

Palm fronds wave their gold
tipped hands ever so slowly
ever so hula slow.

A mongoose darts, swift
from a clump of grasses
then disappears.

Kalaupapa—
north side of nowhere,
a ghost town of souls.

National Memorial Cemetery of the Pacific—Honolulu

Found Grandpa's grave
resting with all the other
military people.

Saucy mynah birds
live by opportunity
boldly unabashed.

Never far from the
sound of the sea—my ear to
the seashell world.

All equal even
near the equator where
sun falls into sea.

Home

Sweet peas riot along
the roadside—deep in their pink
ever after.

Midnight rambler—
fox calls again and again
in the dark hollow.

Vultures tip their wings
on the warm thermals of this
quiet afternoon.

I dreamt of frogs,
throats pulsing in and out,
eyes staring.

Wild tiger lilies
are specific about beauty—
bold orange, freckled.

July

Tiny flying ants
emerge—clouds of white fairies
travel on the breeze.

Ravens careen in
acrobatic pairs over
the river canyon.

A family of
skunks scamper across the road
into the sweet peas.

Fawns jump the road,
darting farther into the woods—
each day a choice.

Cricket chorus in
the bat-dark night of secrets—
I hear an owl call.

Mr. Toad lounges
in the water dish every
darkened evening.

August

Sourdough starter
bubbles in the jar, sweet-sour
ready to rise.

Crickets slow their chorus.
Evening chills the heat of day
in some small measure.

Peppers—sweet and hot
hang like shiny green jewels—
spicy ornaments.

Driving in the dark.
I missed the buck and possum.
Bless them as I pass.

Cricket of the soil—
earth baby, potato bug
home among roots.

Autumn

September

First light. The rooster
calls—once, twice then silence as
winds weave through trees.

This whisper of fall
flows through the night window and
drops to the floor.

Moon peeks like
a giant through a tableau—
black lace pines and cedars.

First rain. Cold morning.
Snow-birds chuff, dance, search
through brown grasses.

The earth gives up the
scent of soil, decaying leaves
with first autumn rains.

Channel strong delight—
gather this change of seasons
to the gate of winter.

Two rough-legged hawks
careen on the wind blue sky,
call and head south.

More and more vultures
tip their wings on the warm winds—
the scent of roadkill.

Gray squirrel running
with a walnut. I slow down.
All is well.

Trees full of vultures
stretching their night-dark wings,
sniffing the air.

October

The river reflects
a thousand mirrors of sunlight
winding down the mountain.

Box turtle prepares
for winter sleep—a sign,
an omen?

Jays squawk, jump from tree
to tree. This morning it's all
about nothing.

Petunias persist.
Their personal beauty
insists on being.

So close, a raven
braids the wind with her black wings—
lights atop a pine.

The acorn seeds send
their roots first to hold fast for
the next generation.

Wind is blustering.
It is raining pine needles—
treetops swirling.

An orange tabby
cries on our doorstep.
Decides to stay.

November

Balmy days, cold nights
fire in the stove, the second
half of dawn wakens.

A tree frog sang at
midday—*sotto voce* its
small announcement.

A squirrel scolds me.
Territorial thing.
I chirp a reply.

Trees weep sap that falls
sticky drops of fine rain
on everything.

Morning star alone
as night retreats across the
ocean to the west.

Winter

December

The cat jumps like a
fox—surprises himself
for no reason at all.

I see you raven,
carving a path through the pines
to a secret place.

Petrichor—that sweet
after-rain smell when earth opens
her hands to heaven.

Chickens fluff feathers,
poke about as soon as sun
warms their chilly yard.

Auspicious day.
Lucky day even with fog,
rain and busyness.

The sun sweeps low
across the horizon, sets
as we lean away.

Wind wakes me, roars through
trees in the hours before
morning breaks cold.

Windstorm—trees crazy
dance and sing a wild song
then it starts to rain.

Raven calls, fluffs her
wings, lowers her head and lifts
off into the west.

Pigs snort for breakfast,
tumble out of bed into
glorious mud.

Tonight the moon is
a bowl of darkness, the stars
witnesses of light.

January

Perhaps this is the
month of sunsets—orange,
firelight red.

White hen scratches
in garden soil with great
vigor—a worm!

A squirrel quarrels
with herself—about what? The
woodpecker may know.

A storm approaches—
gray clouds gather miles high
against the mountains.

It is snowing. Big
flakes of snow cover the ground
with silent white.

Amigo

Old billy goat gruff—
no more suffering.
We let you go.

Frost creeps across
sleeping grasses—sparkles
dead, fallen leaves.

Chickens walk in a
strip of sunshine, hop over
long pine shadows.

I stop to watch
which way the clouds are moving.
It takes a while.

Cedar and oak roast
in the wood stove. I open the
door—sparks jump out.

Gray clouds soften.
Winter shadows of trees stand
bearing the world's weight.

Perched high and safe
a chickaree scolds our cat.
It's a standoff.

Note to gray squirrel:
Do not hesitate. Be quick
about crossing the road.

February

From here—fog curls and
settles on the landscape
intimately.

Morning, mourning dove.
Slow, sad call remembers—each
coo a small comfort.

Winter blue green
as trees embrace underground.
I breathe deeply.

Talking to flowers.
Today it's the only way
to understand.

Chickens fluff and scratch.
They say it's spring, lay their eggs
in secret places.

Spring

March

Windy night until
morning. Trees sing about
the fierce strength of it.

Water is alive.
So, rain talks in its cool ways
to daffodils.

Super moon laces
through oak branches, bright against
a steel blue morning.

A dream about tree
frogs—piles of cool bodies sleeping
with one eye open.

The cat purrs, deep in
sleep, curled against my own half
dreamscape.

My orchids look out
the window at snow falling.
Bloom anyway.

Birds have no idea
we are cloistered since nature
goes ahead with Spring.

The cat purrs, rumbles
content in the rumpled bed
clothes of morning.

Raining steadily.
It's fine, the trees remark,
drinking from their roots.

It is spring because
the crocus pop up—all dark
purple, brilliant.

April

Kay garnu (Nepali)

What to do? Purr like
a cat content to meditate
in this wide moment.

I was talking to
a cedar the other day about
long times ago.

Rain, sleet, thunder
lightning—snow blankets the trees.
Snowplow scrapes by.

Crazy voices in
my dreams until an orange
kitten appears—mew.

A bear visited,
lifted the chain link fence just
like a curtain.

Purple Prince tulips—
four sentinels among
Johnny jump-ups.

Cat creeps forward,
waits for a meadow mouse—
disappointment.

Velvet ants scurry—
marigold orange. Bustle
through dry oak leaves.

May

Peony blossoms
drink sunshine with abandon—
ready to open.

Robin or towhee.
I hear you singing even
when it's at twilight.

A tree frog hides
under the planter box—
sheltering in place.

Coyote scat—
a message on the back road.
An entire story.

Carpenter bees
tease the dog and cat—
just out of reach.

Hens dig dusty holes
in their yard—so deep they
disappear.

Hummingbirds hide in
the big leaf maple, dart and dive,
spar at the feeder.

Time in the garden—
each plant has a story
to tell—I listen.

The petunias
droop when rain falls, stand
up when sun shines.

The breeze swirls pollen—
yellow clouds settle like dust
upon trees, cars, roads,

dogs lying in the sun, cat
prowling through grasses.

A bear in the woods—
no sound, curiosity
breaks the silence.

Rain leaks off trees,
oak leaves so bold with spring—
shining green.

Raven punctuates
the gray sky, irritated
about something.

Bird watching passes
the time as we read field guides
for an answer.

The garden is
thirsty even in the shade.
I wield the hose.

Blue Mountain

Long hike—up and up.
Down the mountain through clouds
of lady beetles.

Lost for a moment
on Blue Mountain—the peak
moves in, out of view.

What a racket!
All the chickens squawking
just after first light.

I check on the hens
to see about the fuss—silence
but for the rooster.

A quail calls—a bit
of laughter this afternoon
ha   ha   ha.

Petunias open
their trumpet blossoms and
make musical colors.

Summer

June

Cicadas hidden
in cedar trees, click a
a simple melody.

The hotter days set
buckeye candelabras
alight in the canyon.

An owl calls, each sound
soft, the repetition soothes
how this day ends.

Full moon hides behind
black stenciled pines. Earth turns
toward morning.

A gray bunny in
my arms—heart purrs, eyes alert,
a soft comfort.

Milkweed begins to
bloom. I examine them for
a Monarch chrysalis.

Sweet pea month—blossoms
cascade their delicate scent
in afternoon warmth.

Shadow insects—earwigs
prowl the dark night in crowds
by the hundreds.

Some rain, thunder,
a stiff breeze between morning
and nightfall.

Goslings clamor, noisy
piping up and down the scale
of learning.

Scent of star jasmine
stirs far and wide in the late
of day—sun half down.

Sweet peas climb through
the garden stealing water as
they can—blush pink.

Earwigs ate the starts
of cucumbers. Earwig month.
Gardener's curse.

First watermelon—
I tap it with my hand as
Uncle advised.

The cat, the dogs lie
flat in the afternoon heat
deep, deeply asleep.

Long day heat wafts up
almost visible waves
in the distance.

Jumping spiders—
small and quick, various
shades of black and white.

There is a time to
water the garden between
flights of mosquitos.

Heat bears down and plants
droop as afternoon sweats
for a breeze.

Brown grasshopper
springs onto a squash leaf.
Summer athlete.

Buttercups among
dry grasses—yellow can
truly shine.

July

Sphinx moths flutter—
white star flowers beckon the
last light of day.

I hear you—raven's
raucous calls careen
higher and higher.

Japanese forest
grass catches midday light—
translucent green.

A screech owl calls
each note bounces down a quick,
soft melody.

Bottoms up—Canada
geese gorge on grasses
under lake water.

Damsel flies skate
just over the surface—
turquoise wings flutter.

Robin bobs his head
runs, stands, warbles, flashes his
rose-colored breast.

Record-breaking heat—
cat stretches on bathroom tiles,
gazes at nothing.

I walk the geese home—
as they thump their water feet
upon the dusty path.

Cumulus clouds
sail miles high, hoard water
in the distance.

Old dog naps deeply
in the summer heat. No dreams
just light snoring.

Koa arrives.
slips into this world—
his own promise.

Evening turns before
midnight, all manner of odors—
animal and earth.

A fox screams danger
back and forth across the draw—
cuts the night air.

In the dusty path
a lion leaves her mark—
a predator's scent.

A tree frog—tiny
hopper in the shadow of
Japanese forest grass.

Quail scurry through
manzanita—each chick swarms
safely with the rest.

I heard the owl last
night drop his call—a fall of
dark melody.

Two jays tantalize,
harangue our cat who flicks the
tip of his tail.

A mantis perched on
my blueberry basket, turns
her head—a question?

Midnight visitor—
black bear rummages in the barn.
Just dry chicken feed.

Stellar's jay out of
the nest—not ready to fly.
Cry baby.

Who else knows morning
as well as the rooster and
his bevy of hens?

Do crickets wait in
trees to measure time in the
twilight of evening?

Senryu

In the wee hours there
is no dreaming, just one thought
after another.

Poised for friendship—we
counted on time enough
to share the amazing.

Words flutter as if
to make a poem or song
or nothing at all.

Whenever light
lifts in waves of early sun—
my poem laughs.

Quiet and quiet.
Unintended consequences.
What is there to say?

Circumstantial
evidence is enough
to answer why.

Optimism
arm wrestles despair as if
the world depends on it.

What ifs can worry.
Maybe is not a promise.
Perhaps is a problem?

Gratitude lingers,
overrides false expectations
in the kindest way.

In the after-words
of our conversation—
I'm thinking.

Where is the hundredth
monkey? Waits for us to
notice—it's time.

Patriotism
and independence suffer
fools quietly.

The aftermath of
continuous dreaming—
bouts of confusion.

In the absence of
reason, what is left to do
but call for truth.

Radio today.
Alone in the studio.
No grievous errors.

Sadness swallows me
whole, settles in my stomach
like a parasite.

It is perhaps a
small thing—what we give the world—
a taste of kindness.

If I could untangle
these fevered dreams—each one real
in its own way.

A quiet day of
choices. My gray hair sweeps
across the years.

Gratitude must not
hide—life is too short for the
grace that goes with it.

A meal outside with
book friends until mosquitoes
arrive for dessert.

I am sorry for
several things that prove
my imperfections.

My brain talking to
itself—not in a good way—
more like obsessing.

I closed my eyes as
chanting took your soul away
and thought I might fly.

That ship has sailed—yes
again and again   bon voyage.
We agree life is short.

I comb the distance
between your passing and
my loneliness.

How do I gather
the threads of my life into
some kind of order?

Eighteen years ago
we watched, held our collective
breath, then prayed for peace.

In the aftermath
of the news I search for kindness
to protest cruelty.

Depression is a
transient state of waiting
for some relief.

Truth withheld is
as good as a bald-faced lie
when it matters most.

I awoke to the
loss of objective truth and
wondered—what now?

I try to avoid
the news as everyone is
divided by two.

My blood is full of
words—rusty red with longing
and the urge to sing.

I make my way back,
step between memories for
the one full of joy.

Time collides with the
future in alarming ways.
I try to keep up.

Clutter approaches
the tipping point of chaos—
now I attack.

Everyone makes a
promise right now—I say make
it small enough to keep.

In friendship
we open our baggage and
compare sorrows.

Unfortunately
we find ourselves trapped—the world
living in bad faith.

We throw words around
freely and with quiet intent—
a room of poets.

How closely we listen
to each other. Life depends
on these moments.

I keep sighing deep
sighs one after another.
Breathing for relief.

Lethargy is a word
that sounds like it feels and
feels like it sounds.

In the aftermath
of the debates, can we agree
this is hard, hard times?

Who is king of the
world now? A virus so small
it flies on a breath.

The darker hours breathe—
silence being the master
of repetitious dreams.

Molokai

Long day of travel
trials, irritations—a test
of deep patience.

Kona

Everything slows down
here on the island,
I skid to a stop.

(Sorry)

Kala mai for us,
the two-leggeds who bumble
toward the future.

A final farewell
to this parallel life,
to my island self.

I fight through a fog
of lethargy with a small
sword of gratitude.

Reading by the fire—
the wood stove crackling with heat,
sheltering in place.

Parallel world of
ordinary dreams. I live
both lives equally.

Before and after.
All tomorrows and lives
measured against now.

Laughing buddha
opens his arms wide—begs
to be remembered.

Angel memories—
nubs of my wings itch
to fly in dreams.

Low thoughts scatter
like broken dreams before
morning cracks open.

Every day is like
every other day. I
wake to remember.

On the other side
of this pandemic what shall
we find? Compassion?

Hard—the willpower
to avoid the news. Like a
moth to a flame.

Inhabit silence—
that long, lost friend left behind
when life was busy.

Before nature was
my observation point—now
global pandemic.

Herd immunity
contact tracing, homemade masks—
good morning today.

John Prine

By evening a poet
dies—his words hang in the air
cycling through clouds.

When everyday feels
like Sunday—that sad feeling
much like a gray sky.

We have stepped into
the dystopian now—
middle of the tale.

Dream of making masks.
Half asleep I design masks.
Awake—I sew masks.

In some true way we
live with contradictions—
paradox worlds.

Spring cleaning evolves
in the shadow of waiting—
the dust of years.

The mind, susceptible
to the whims of the body—
runs like a monkey.

Time as string theory
alone in the universe
of curious worlds.

Only some
in these uncertain times
expect deadlines.

Fantasy will be
a return to normal.
Apocalypse now.

I read the news and
become lost in stray thoughts—
not in a good way.

It could be today
or tomorrow but today
is every day.

A special meal—
food memories sweet and sour,
melancholy, too.

My body wants to
rest more often now—keep
moving—I say.

How often must
compassion elude the many
before we learn.

In those times, these times
it is a shame to notice—
violently the same.

The privacy of
loneliness weighs heaviest
just before morning.

Don't be distracted
just because it's happened before
and nothing changed.

Division is a
kind of subtraction—separates
reason from wisdom.

This week feels like next
week while every day is
any day like another.

The world wearies me—
body, mind, and soul—tired to
the core where joy hides.

Absolutes are reserved
for facts especially when faced
with uncertainty.

History unfolds
in real time. No take backs for
the wrong decision.

Analysis:
The right side of history
is a moral issue.

Opinion:
What I believe based upon
facts, reality.

Comfort can be
a single observation—
bird on the wing.

Low thoughts scatter
like broken dreams before
morning cracks open.

The underlying
meaning abhors platitudes,
casual attention.

Kombucha in my
father's beer glass—the gold trim
slightly tarnished now.

Lethargy is
depression dressed up as a
midnight metaphor.

My body hums and not
in a good way—anxiety
in all my cells.

Peace in mind, peace out
just within comprehension—
a difficulty.

How many people
pray for the common good?
Not enough.

People quick to
write the narrative
tend to be lying.

Search for the truth—
now everything is suspect.
Too much information.

After Words

I call the following Haiku Questions—which I wrote one summer day, August 2020. They were written in one hour. This is how I breathe in syllables and think in them as well.

They are a combination of haiku (the traditional form about nature) and senryu (about people and present time and events), since while a poet may be attuned to the natural world, we cannot be oblivious to the foibles of humanity.

What if this were the
day we could finally rest
in normality?

How will it sound—
the truth ringing like a
grandfather clock?

When we hazard a
guess about what matters most?
Who is listening?

Are exceptions to
the rule compatible with
the Golden Rule?

In the event that
we can't remember how
it happened—what then?

What is there inside
the dream of reality
upside down?

Is there some kind of
alchemy between then and
now and permanence?

Can contributions
to the inevitable
defy gravity?

Will finding how stars
resolve darkness be as
good as string theory?

To the power of
ten times ten—why do beliefs
explode like that?

Is this where we wait—
listening for the echoes
of sanity?

If we concocted
a story to make real—
would it be kind?

I heard a frog sing.
What else is there to
know in this world?

If you could fly—
how high, how far, how swift
would the journey be?

The day is low, low.
I despair of people.
What to do?

The dog naps in my
lap. What simple dreams does
she see, smell?

What makes this complete?
A distant wind climbing the
mountains—tree by tree?

Turning the ship on
a dime. Who says it takes so
long? Worth a try.

As silence gathers
in the long dark hours—
how long to linger?

Sure, you've wondered—
is suffering a choice or
a false option?

A squirrel chatters,
throws pinecones from the treetops.
Who is the target?

Early and forceful—
which is the path that leads to
common sense?

House spiders build and
rebuild their webs—catching dust,
maybe a moth or two?

Will a map to the
next universe comply
with this urgency?

What if we saw each
other standing between this
life and the next?

Are imprints of small
injuries the scars we
share with true friends?

Is there a house for
everyone left behind or
do we abandon them?

Do no harm.
Is there a medication
for negativity?

Do we have the
discipline to listen?
Can there be one song?

Why is this the year
of one calamity and
then another?

What transcends time
more than how we inhabit
the unusual?

How can I stop the
repetition of sorrows
so deeply hidden?

I'm looking for a
word, a remedy, a poem.
Where is that fortune?

Is the treasure of
life measured by a clock
or memories?

Do answers have
questions in the same sense of
wayward thinking?

Is the frequency
of beauty forgotten
along with ourselves?

How does raven
hide from the heat of summer
being dark as night?

Bibliography

Addiss, Stephen, with Fumiko and Akira Yamamoto. *A Haiku Menagerie: Living Creatures in Poems and Prints.* Weatherhill, 1992.

Basho, Matsuo. *The Narrow Road to Oku* translated by Donald Keene and illustrated by kiri-e artist Miyata Masayuki. Kodansha, 2017.

Blyth, R. H. *Zen in English Literature and Oriental Classics.* Angelico Press, 2016.

Britton, Dorothy (translator). *A Haiku Journey: Basho's Narrow Road to a Far Province.* Kodansha International, 1974.

Chi, Lu. *Wen Fu: The Art of Writing*, translated by Sam Hamill. Milkweed Editions, 2000.

Collins, Billy. *She Was Just Seventeen.* Modern Haiku Press, 2006.

Cooper, Arthur (translator). *Li Po Tu Fu.* Penguin Books, 1973.

Cuneo, Louis. *haiku revisited*. Celestial Arts, 1975.

Donegan, Patricia. *haiku mind: 108 Poems to Cultivate Awareness & Open Your Heart*. Shambala, 2010.

Donegan, Patricia and Yoshie Ishibasi. *Chiyo-ni: Woman Haiku Master*. Tuttle Publishing, 1998.

---. *Haiku People: Big and Small in Poems and Prints*. Weatherhill, 1998.

Hamill, Sam (translator). *Narrow Road to the Interior and other writings of Matsuo Basho*. Shambala Classics, 2000.

Harrison, Jim and Ted Koozer. *Braided Creek: A Conversation in Poetry*. Copper Canyon Press, 2003.

Hass, Robert (editor). *The Essential Haiku: Versions of Basho, Buson, & Issa*. The Ecco Press, 1994.

Henderson, Harold G. *An Introduction to Haiku: An Anthology of Poems and Poets from Basho to Shiki*. Doubleday, Anchor Books, 1958.

Higginson, William J. *The Haiku Seasons: Poetry of the Natural World*. Kodansha International, 1996.

Hirshfield, Jane. *The Heart of Haiku: Kindle Single. Haiku.* translations by Hirshfield and Mariko Aratani. Amazon.com, 2011.

Kerouac, Jack. *Book of Haikus*. Penguin Books 2003.

Koren, Leonard. *Wabi-Sabi for Artists, Poets, & Philosophers*. Imperfect Publishing 2008.

Levering, Miriam. *Zen: Images, Texts, and Teachings*. Artisan Workman Publishing Company, 2000.

Lowenstein, Tom. *Haiku Inspirations: Poems and Meditations on Nature and Beauty*. Duncan Baird Publishers, 2006.

Merton, Thomas. *The Way of Chuang Tzu*. New Directions, 1969.

Mullen, Harryette. *Urban Tumbleweed: Notes from a Tanka Diary*. Graywolf Press, 2013.

Rexroth, Kenneth. One Hundred Poems from the Japanese. New Directions 1964.

Rexroth, Kenneth with Ling Chung. Women Poets of China. New Directions 1972.

Ueda, Makoto. *Modern Japanese Tanka*. Columbia University Press, 1996.

Vanden Heuvel (editor). *The Haiku Anthology*. W. W. Norton, 1999.

Watson, Burton (translator). *Poems of a Mountain Home: Saigyo*. Columbia University Press, 1991.

---. *Ryokan: Zen Monk-Poet of Japan*. Columbia University Press, 1977.

Wright, Richard. *Haiku: The Last Poems of an American Icon*. Arcade Publishing, 2012.

Young, David (translator). *Moon Woke Me Up Nine Times: Selected haiku of Basho*. Alfred A. Knopf, 2018.

Yuasa, Nobuyuki. *Basho: The Narrow Road to the Deep North and other Travel Sketches*. Penguin Classes, 1966.

---. Issa: *The Year of My Life*. University of California Press, 1972.

Picture Books

Gianferrari, Maria. *Whoo-ku Haiku: A Great Horned Owl Story*. GP Putnam, 2020.

Gollub, Matthew (story and translations). *Cool Melons—Turn to Frogs!: The Life and Poems of Issa*. Lee & Low Books, 1998.

Higginson, William (editor), illustrator Sandra Speidel. *Wind in the Long Grass*. Simon & Schuster, 1991.

Lewis, Richard (editor), illustrator Ezra jack Keats. *In a Spring Garden*. Dial Books for Young Readers, 1965.

Mannis, Celeste Davidson, with pictures by Susan Kathleen Hartung. *One Leaf Rides the Wind*. Viking, 2002.

Myers, Tim. *Basho and the Fox*. Marshall Cavendish, 2000.

Prelutsky, Jack. *If Not for the Cat: Haiku*, paintings by Ted Rand. HarperCollins Children's Books, 2004.

Ramirez-Christensen, Esperanza, illustrated by Tracy Gallup. *My First Book of Haiku Poems: A Picture, a Poem and a Dream.* Tuttle Publishing, 2019.

Reibstein, Mark and Ed Young Illustrator. *Wabi Sabi.* Little Brown Books for Young Readers, 2008.

Shannon, George (editor), paintings by Malcah Zeldis. *Spring: A Haiku Story.* Greenwillow Books, 1996.

Sidman, Joyce. Illustrator Beckie Prange. *Song of the Boatman & other pond poems.* Houghton Mifflin, 2005.

Spivak, Dawnine. *Grass Sandals: The Travels of Basho.* Atheneum, 1997.

Students of St. Mary's Catholic School (Mansfield, MA). *Haiku Hike.* Scholastic, Inc., 2005.

About the Author

Linda Toren lives in the foothills of Calaveras County with her husband Theo, dogs, a cat, and many chickens.

Linda is a retired teacher and currently director of *Voices of Wisdom* through Manzanita Writer's Press (MWP). She has presented poetry workshops for children and adults—publishing schoolwide collections of poetry and art at local elementary schools for more than 15 years.

Her poetry appears in the following collections *Manzanita: Poetry and Prose of the Mother Lode & Sierra* (MWP 1995–2008), *Wild Edges* (MWP 2013) *Wine, Cheese & Chocolate* (MWP 2014), *Voices of Wisdom* (MWP 2018, 2019), *Out of the Fire* (MWP 2017), *Teaching with Fire (Poetry That Sustains the Courage to Teach)* by Sam M. Intrator & Megan Scribner, editors (2003), *CollisionV: an Intersection of Poetry and Photography* (2018).

Linda produces a community radio program at KQBM Blue Mountain radio which streams live at KQBM.org. Archived shows can be found at archive.org. Search for "Way with Words" Linda Toren. It's a program dedicated to poetry, prose, nonfiction, literary news, lyrics and the celebration of thoughts and language.

www.ingramcontent.com/pod-product-compliance
Lightning Source LLC
Chambersburg PA
CBHW030438010526
44118CB00011B/695
9780996885867